LEGO

MIGHTY LEGO® MECHS

Written by Julia March

DK

CONTENTS

CHAPTER 1
SHARP SHOOTERS

Why go toe-to-toe with an enemy when you can flatten them from afar with a well-aimed missile? Shooters are among a LEGO® mech's most useful weapons. Some mechs even keep them folded away until needed, giving foes a sneaky surprise. Ready, aim... fire!

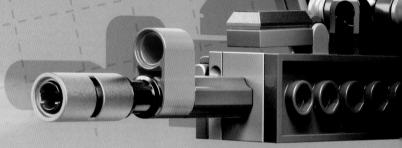

CAUTION

FIRE MECH STATS

Theme	THE LEGO® NINJAGO® MOVIE™			
Set name	Fire Mech 70615			
Pieces	944			
Released	2017			
Fought	Lord Garmadon's Shark Army			

Weapons	▮ ▮ ▮ ▮ ▮
Defence	▮ ▮ ▮ ▯ ▯
Agility	▮ ▮ ▮ ▯ ▯
Speed	▮ ▮ ▮ ▯ ▯

Proud samurai flags

Arms end in powerful fire blasters

Ninjago symbols on fire tanks

Flexible fuel pipes

Kai views battle from cockpit

Bendable knee joints

Kai uses another mech in 71720 Fire Stone Mech in 2020. That one is half red, half grey because he shares it with Cole.

KAI'S FIRE MECH

Red alert! Garmadon's Shark Army is invading the streets of Ninjago City. Ninja Kai goes blazing into action in his scarlet Fire Mech, determined to put the heat on those fishy foes. The posable mech has an array of weapons, including twin disk shooters powerful enough to send any fish flying.

Shoulder-mounted disk shooters

MMM, MY FAVOURITE... FRIED FISH!

Wide feet help with balance – and add stomp power!

THIS MECH IS **9** MINIFIGURES TALL!

EEK... I'M SHAKING LIKE A JELLYFISH!

Samurai X blade detaches from holster on back

Mech is over 15 cm (5 in) tall, but blade worn on back increases height by 8cm (3 in).

AH, KILLOW... I'VE BEEN X-PECTING YOU!

Samurai X symbol on chest

Wrist-mounted stud shooters

Whirling blade hand

Super long lower legs give agility

Slim, jointed ankles for sudden turns

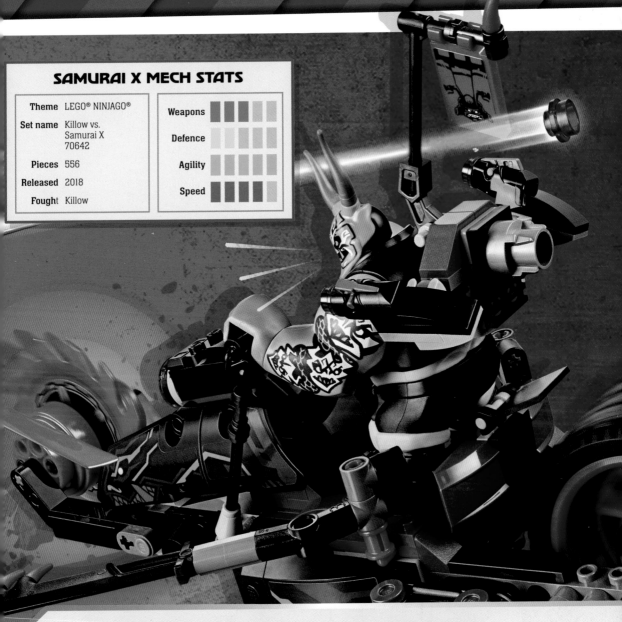

SAMURAI X MECH STATS

Theme	LEGO® NINJAGO®	
Set name	Killow vs. Samurai X 70642	
Pieces	556	
Released	2018	
Fought	Killow	

Weapons

Defence

Agility

Speed

SAMURAI X MECH

When the Samurai X mech meets Killow's Oni Chopper, expect an all-out battle involving katanas, clubs and wrist-mounted stud shooters. While Killow tears up the road on his Oni Chopper, Samurai X just has to decide whether to use her mech's rotating blade, shooters or twin swords to stop him in his tracks!

MECH FILE

Theme	LEGO® NINJAGO®
Set	Garma Mecha Man 70613
Pieces	747
Released	2017

Shark fin cockpit cover

Hinged cockpit lined with shark teeth

Long shoulder pieces resemble shark fins

WAAAH... TWO AGAINST ONE? NOT FAIR!

Movable fingers on right hand

Shark ammo belt connected to fish tank

THE GARMA MECHA MAN IS TALLER THAN THE FIRE STONE MECH, BUT HAS MUCH SHORTER LEGS.

Jointed hips allow legs to splay

Huge, flat feet

BATTLE STATS

Name: Garma Mech Man
Height: 30 cm (11 in)
Ammo tank capacity: 5/10
Laser power: 5/10
Missiles: 0/10
Blaster power: 7/10
Battle rating: 7/10

Name: Fire Stone Mech
Height: 27 cm (10 in)
Blade power: 7/10
Missiles: 6/10
Stride length: 8/10
Armour: 7/10
Battle rating: 8/10

FIRE STONE MECH VS. GARMA MECHA MAN

Meet the Garma Mecha Man… Garmadon's first mech. It's got a laser beam, spears and a fiendishly fishy shark blaster. Garmadon is gleefully rushing into battle, but oh… what's this striding towards him? It's the Fire Stone Mech, driven by Ninja Kai and Cole working in tandem. That's double trouble, and it might turn Garmadon's plans to rubble.

COCKPIT HAS ROOM FOR TWO – KAI AT THE CONTROLS AND COLE BEHIND HIM.

Shoulders rotate 360 degrees

Stone pauldron

ALL FIRED UP, GARMADON? YOU SOON WILL BE!

Twin stud shooters on hand

Elbows bend backwards as well as forwards

Huge, stomping feet able to rotate

Stone hand has two fingers and a thumb

MECH FILE

Theme	LEGO® NINJAGO®
Set	Fire Stone Mech 71720
Pieces	968
Released	2020

BASTION

Meet Bastion, a relic of an omnic army that once menaced the world. The revived robot now wanders peacefully through nature... until his battle programming kicks back in. Then he flips, reconfiguring to sentry mode and back again in moments. Gatling gun or mini gun, that is the question...

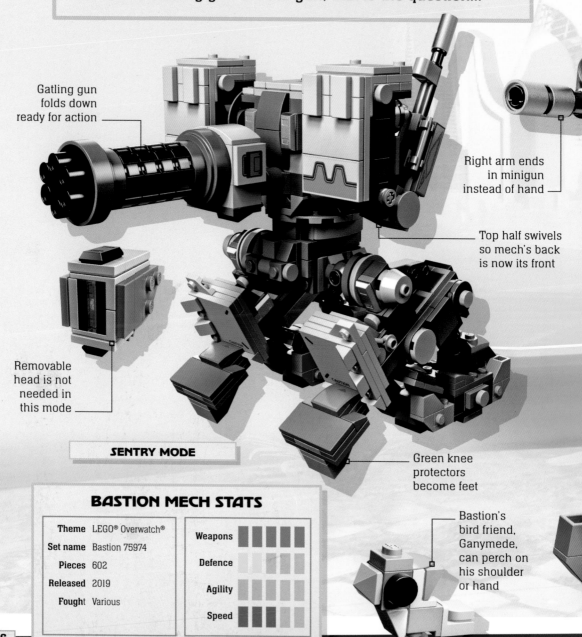

Gatling gun folds down ready for action

Right arm ends in minigun instead of hand

Top half swivels so mech's back is now its front

Removable head is not needed in this mode

SENTRY MODE

Green knee protectors become feet

Bastion's bird friend, Ganymede, can perch on his shoulder or hand

BASTION MECH STATS

Theme	LEGO® Overwatch®
Set name	Bastion 75974
Pieces	602
Released	2019
Fought	Various

Weapons	▪▪▪▪▪
Defence	▪▪
Agility	▪▪
Speed	▪▪▪

Red light brick is turned on by stud at the back

BEEP...
BEEP...
BEEEEEEEEEP

Bastion is an E54 omnic; a superior model to the more usual B73s.

Top half of mech swivels at the waist

Wrist rotates and fingers open, close and spread out

In recon mode Bastion is 26 cm (10 in) tall. In sentry mode he folds down to 17cm (6 in).

"Caution" stickers warn curious strangers to stay away

Big, sturdy feet rotate and tilt for added stability.

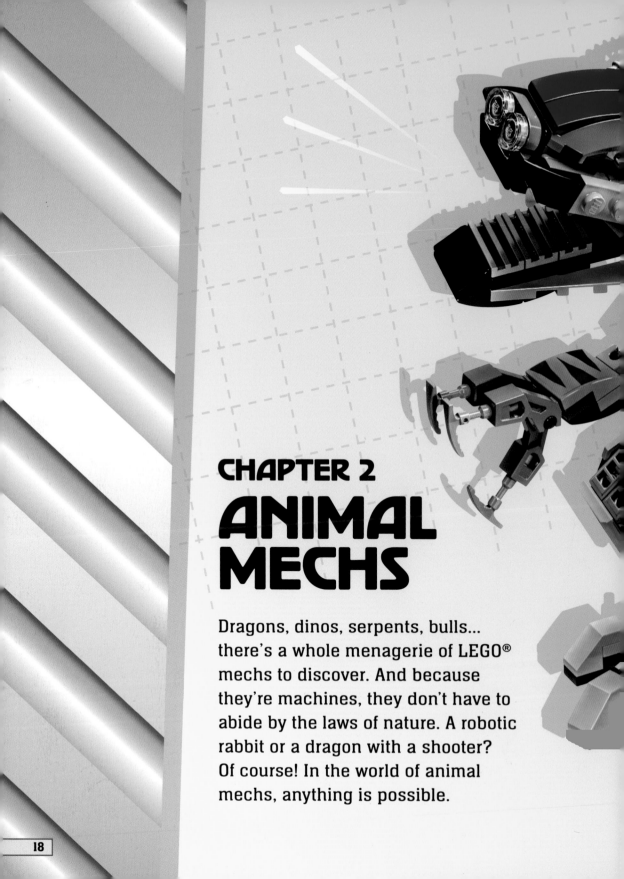

CHAPTER 2
ANIMAL MECHS

Dragons, dinos, serpents, bulls... there's a whole menagerie of LEGO® mechs to discover. And because they're machines, they don't have to abide by the laws of nature. A robotic rabbit or a dragon with a shooter? Of course! In the world of animal mechs, anything is possible.

D.VA MECH

D.Va once made a living as a video gamer. Now she's playing a new and bigger game – defending South Korea against giant sentient robots called omnics. Her mech is rabbit-shaped, and it's just as bouncy as a real rabbit. In the cockpit, D.Va has one aim in mind – to make life hard for the omnics. Fire up those fusion cannons!

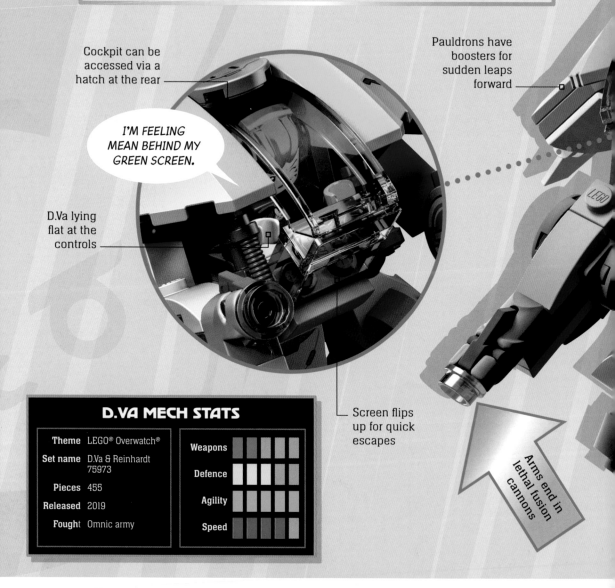

Cockpit can be accessed via a hatch at the rear

Pauldrons have boosters for sudden leaps forward

I'M FEELING MEAN BEHIND MY GREEN SCREEN.

D.Va lying flat at the controls

Screen flips up for quick escapes

Arms end in lethal fusion cannons

D.VA MECH STATS

Theme	LEGO® Overwatch®					
Set name	D.Va & Reinhardt 75973					
Pieces	455					
Released	2019					
Fought	Omnic army					

Weapons	▢	▢	▢	▢	▢
Defence	▢	▢	▢	▢	▢
Agility	▢	▢	▢	▢	▢
Speed	▢	▢	▢	▢	▢

HA! MY RABBIT MECH HAS GOT YOU JUMPING!

The top of the mech shows off colourful sticker ads for D.Va's sponsors.

Movable thrusters

The letters "MEKA" on D.Va's mech stand for "Mobile Exoforce of the Korean Army."

Sturdy knees fixed at a 90° angle for strength

Ratcheted hips for nimble, omnic-dodging sidesteps

Rabbitlike feet and springy ankles

Heels and toes swivel to aid stability in all poses

EMPIRE DRAGON

Evil Unagami has flown into town on his Empire Dragon! This hi-tech beast has stud shooters in its shoulders, digi blade wings and a katana on the end of its tail. Its sharp claws are ready to take a swipe at any ninja that comes too close! Unagami sits at the control board in the cockpit. Can the ninja find a way to bring Unagami down?

Windshield protects Unagami in the cockpit

Head has a sharp blade as a topknot!

TOP VIEW

Snapping jaws can crunch ninja

TIME TO POWER DOWN, UNAGAMI!

YOU'LL NEVER GET PAST MY EMPIRE DRAGON!

Stud shooters can be angled up or down

Digi blades can slice through the air for fast flying

The Empire Dragon is an expression of Unagami's anger. No wonder its eyes glow an angry red!

Tail is jointed, allowing it to swish and swat away attacks from the rear

Sturdy feet attach to legs with ball joints for flexibility

THE EMPIRE DRAGON IS 39 CM (15 IN) LONG.

EMPIRE DRAGON STATS

		Weapons					
Theme	LEGO® NINJAGO®						
Set name	Empire Dragon 71713	Defence					
Pieces	286	Agility					
Released	2020	Speed					
Fought	Kai and Lloyd						

MECH FILE

Theme	LEGO® Jurassic World
Set	T. rex vs Dino-Mech Battle 75938
Pieces	716
Released	2019

Powerful jaws make quick work of prey

THE T. REX IS PROTECTED BY ITS TOUGH, SCALY SKIN.

Metal grid instead of teeth

Curved talons to claw enemies

Three sharp metal claws can grip prey

Muscular legs stabilize the T. rex's body

BATTLE STATS

Name: T. rex
Height: 11 cm (4 in)
Jaw power: 10/10
Missiles: 0/10
Grab power: 4/00
Brute strength: 9/10
Battle rating: 8/10

Name: Dino-Mech
Height: 14 cm (5 in)
Jaw power: 7/10
Missiles: 0/10
Grab power: 8/10
Armour: 6/10
Battle rating: 7/10

T. REX VS. DINO-MECH!

Scary, glowing eyes

Headlights illuminate the mech's target

Bad guy Danny Nedermeyer is on the rampage in his fearsome Dino-Mech! With its mechanical jaws, glowing eyes and clutching steel claws, it is a powerful prehistoric mech. But is it a match for a real T. rex?

WATCH MY MECH TURN THIS T. REX INTO A T. WRECK!

The Dino-Mech is an impressive foe, but its long arm is an easy target for a mighty T. rex chomp!

WATCH OUT FOR THE DINO-MECH'S THRASHING MECHANICAL TAIL!

Posable legs with protective armour

GREEN NINJA MECH DRAGON

Lord Garmadon never gives up! He's invading Ninjago City again, but look out… the Green Ninja is waiting for him in his Dragon Mech. With its posable body, this dragon poses a problem for even the wickedest of warlords. Can Garmadon dodge its snapping jaws? Will its swishing tail send him into a tailspin? And how about those leg mounted stud-shooters? Go, Green Ninja!

OUCH… YOU NEED TO MUZZLE THAT MECH!

The Dragon Mech's eye details are made up of golden bananas and jagged axe blades.

Trans-green cockpit screen

Golden whiskers can be angled up or down.

Snapping jaw with movable tongue

Tail ends in golden flame

Spines along body and tail can be raised and lowered

GREEN NINJA MECH DRAGON STATS

Theme	THE LEGO® NINJAGO® MOVIE™	
Set name	Green Ninja Mech Dragon 70612	
Pieces	544	
Released	2017	
Fought	Shark Army Gunner	

Weapons	
Defence	
Agility	
Speed	

CAN WE MAKE IT SNAPPY? IT'S NEARLY TEATIME!

PREPARE TO LOSE THAT LASER, GARMADON.

Swishing tail activated by wheel

From nose to tail, this mech is an amazing 60 cm (23 in) long.

Neck raises and lowers and head rotates

Legs can fold parallel with body for flight mode

Two slashing claws on each foot

WE DON'T CARE IF YOU WHACK US DOWN, NINJA!

...WE JUST JUMP ON OUR HEALTH BOARDS FOR A NEW LIFE!

Wings connect to barrel-shaped engines that tilt

Game-style controls in cockpit

Toes move individually

The Cyber Dragon shines bright! Its fangs, wings, spines, and tail tips are fluorescent green.

JAY'S CYBER DRAGON STATS

Theme	LEGO® NINJAGO®
Set name	Jay's Cyber Dragon 71711
Pieces	518
Released	2020
Fought	Unagami and the Whack Rats

Weapons	
Defence	
Agility	
Speed	

JAY'S CYBER DRAGON

There's everything to play for! Digi Jay and Digi Nya are in Prime Empire, battling Unagami and the Whack Rats. Can Jay's Cyber Dragon give the Ninja the edge? Its dazzling trans-green wings can befuddle a bad guy, and its spring-loaded shooters can give a Whack Rat a nasty whack. Game on!

Big, white ears fold up or down

Jointed tail lashes from side to side

From nose to tail, Jay's Cyber Dragon measures 39 cm (15 in).

MY WEAPONS MAKE ME A MASTER HACKER...

Two knifelike fangs in lower jaw

Two spring-loaded shooters in chest

FRONT VIEW

TIME TO DELETE YOU, NINJA!

NINDROID MECHDRAGON

Master Wu has turned evil and has teamed up with the nindroids! Together they are riding into battle on the Nindroid MechDragon. This dragon-shaped mech is an intimidating machine, boasting circular saws in its shoulders and sharp blades on each wing. It even has two detachable flyers so the Nindroids can attack from all angles. It'll take teamwork to fend off this foe!

Enough room in its jaws for a ninja!

One of eight katana blades

The MechDragon can stand up on its hind legs to display its full height. Enough to strike fear into the heart of any ninja!

STANDING VIEW

Missile fired from cannon mounted on back

YAWN... YOUR ANTICS ARE DRAGGIN' ON, WU!

This car belongs to Nya – hopefully Lloyd returns it in one piece!

Theme	LEGO® NINJAGO®	Weapons					
Set name	Nindroid MechDragon 70725	Defence					
Pieces	691	Agility					
Released	2014	Speed					
Fought	Lloyd and Sensei Garmadon						

TAKE THAT, PUNY NINJA!

Tail ends in a tusk piece

Nindroid operates cannon

Three posable claws on feet

Circular saw spins with the turn of a gear

CHAPTER 3
MINI MECHS

Don't underestimate small mechs. That's a big mistake! Mini mechs can't make the battlefield shake or tower over enemies, but they have speed and agility on their side. They often have an arsenal of cunningly creative weapons, too. From mini mechs, mighty victories are born.

BUFFMILLION MECH

The Ninja are flying in to rescue Kai and Nya's parents from Dragon's Forge... but they are in for a sneaky, snaky surprise. A giant Buffmillion mech is guarding the Forge. It has four watchful heads that sway left and right, and posable arms for knocking down intruders. The Ninja must beat this buffed-up boa, or they could soon be hissstory!

Fingers made of red horns and tail tips

Molded, fixed elbows do not bend

Crest looks like snakes rearing to strike

THIS SMALL MECH STANDS AT JUST 12 CM (4 IN) TALL.

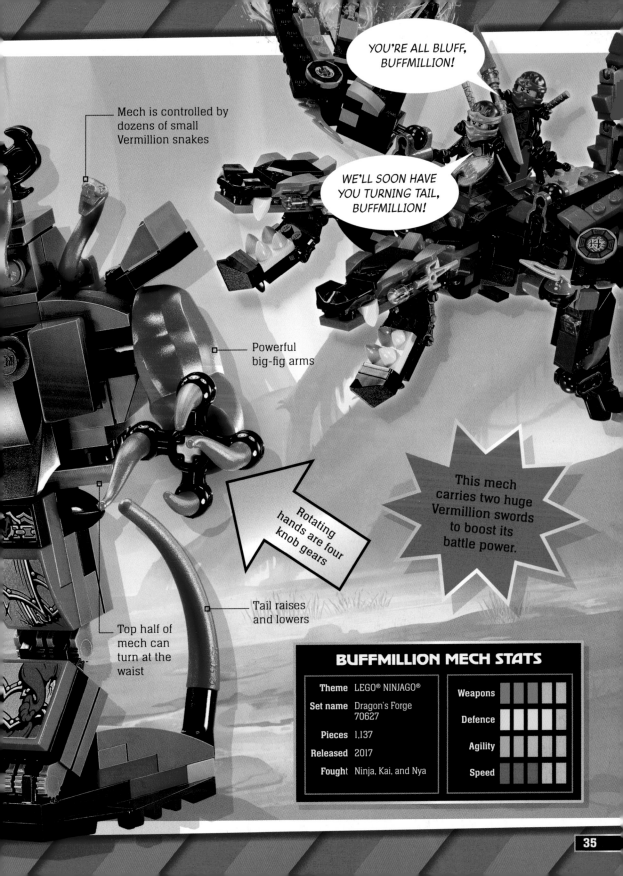

Mech is controlled by dozens of small Vermillion snakes

YOU'RE ALL BLUFF, BUFFMILLION!

WE'LL SOON HAVE YOU TURNING TAIL, BUFFMILLION!

Powerful big-fig arms

Rotating hands are four knob gears

This mech carries two huge Vermillion swords to boost its battle power.

Tail raises and lowers

Top half of mech can turn at the waist

BUFFMILLION MECH STATS

Theme	LEGO® NINJAGO®
Set name	Dragon's Forge 70627
Pieces	1,137
Released	2017
Fought	Ninja, Kai, and Nya

Weapons				
Defence				
Agility				
Speed				

JAY'S ELECTRO MECH

Eyezor has Jay in his sights but yikes…the Ninja is in his Electro Mech. It strides powerfully on sturdy legs, a whirling shuriken blade in its left hand and a swishing sword in its right. It has two more golden blades on its back, too. Can Eyezor's cannon car bash this bulky blue mech, or will Jay deal the villain a slice of justice?

YOU JUST DON'T MAKE THE CUT, JAY

Sword is identical to the two on mech's back

This compact mech is 12 cm (4 in) tall. With its arms and weapons outstretched, it is wider than it is tall, at 16cm (6.5 in) wide.

MECH AT REST

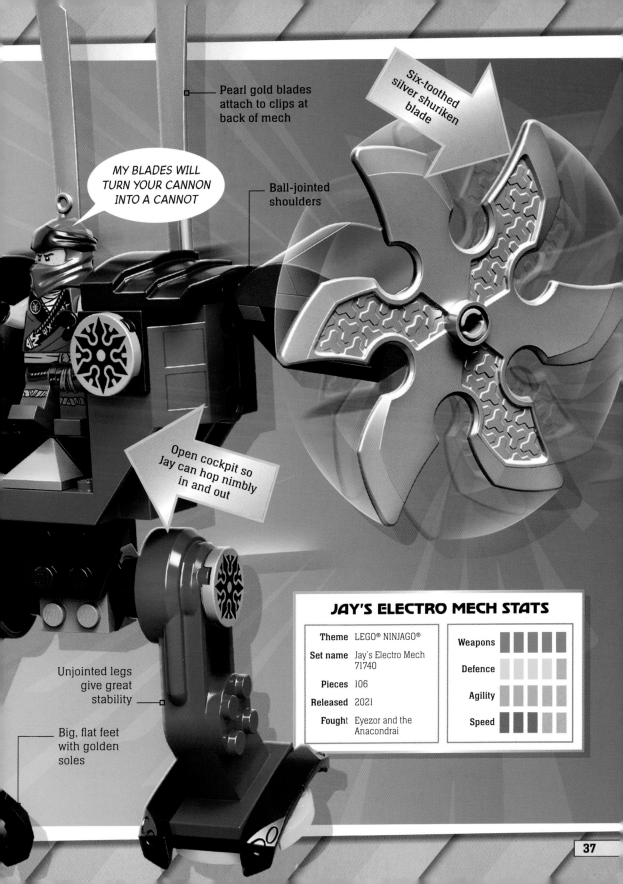

Pearl gold blades attach to clips at back of mech

Six-toothed silver shuriken blade

MY BLADES WILL TURN YOUR CANNON INTO A CANNOT

Ball-jointed shoulders

Open cockpit so Jay can hop nimbly in and out

Unjointed legs give great stability

Big, flat feet with golden soles

JAY'S ELECTRO MECH STATS

Theme	LEGO® NINJAGO®
Set name	Jay's Electro Mech 71740
Pieces	106
Released	2021
Fought	Eyezor and the Anacondrai

Weapons	
Defence	
Agility	
Speed	

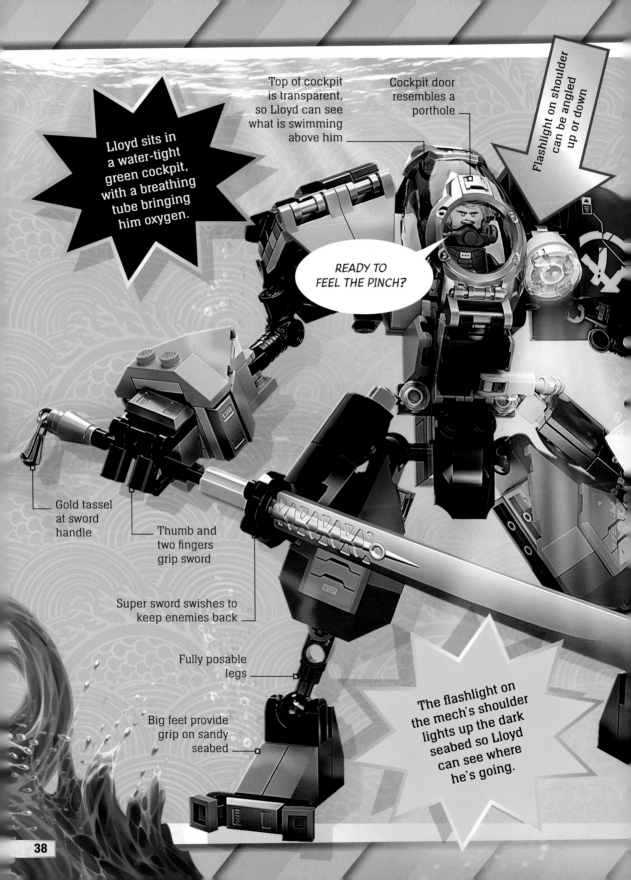

Top of cockpit is transparent, so Lloyd can see what is swimming above him

Cockpit door resembles a porthole

Flashlight on shoulder can be angled up or down

Lloyd sits in a water-tight green cockpit, with a breathing tube bringing him oxygen.

READY TO FEEL THE PINCH?

Gold tassel at sword handle

Thumb and two fingers grip sword

Super sword swishes to keep enemies back

Fully posable legs

Big feet provide grip on sandy seabed

The flashlight on the mech's shoulder lights up the dark seabed so Lloyd can see where he's going.

LLOYD'S HYDRO MECH

The Endless Sea is looking choppy today. Far below the surface, Lloyd is striding into battle in his Hydro Mech. He's determined to grab the precious wave amulet from the eel-like Maaray Guard. Look out for the mech's hydraulic claw – it's bigger than any crab's, and it's poised to close in on the prize when Lloyd hits the controls. SNAP!

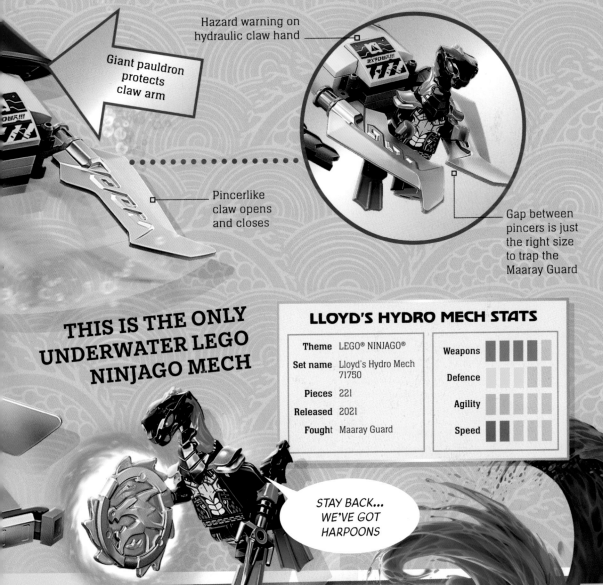

Hazard warning on hydraulic claw hand

Giant pauldron protects claw arm

Pincerlike claw opens and closes

Gap between pincers is just the right size to trap the Maaray Guard

THIS IS THE ONLY UNDERWATER LEGO NINJAGO MECH

LLOYD'S HYDRO MECH STATS

Theme	LEGO® NINJAGO®
Set name	Lloyd's Hydro Mech 71750
Pieces	221
Released	2021
Fought	Maaray Guard

Weapons	
Defence	
Agility	
Speed	

STAY BACK... WE'VE GOT HARPOONS

OMNIC BASTION

Poor Bastion! The lonely omnic is no longer at war with humans, but his battle programming just keeps kicking in. When that happens he switches between gatling-blasting sentry and handgun-wielding recon modes. Humans often set Bastion off, so he avoids them. It's safer to wander through nature with Ganymede, his bird companion.

The display stand bears the name of the Overwatch creators, Blizzard. Ganymede sits on Bastion's shoulder.

Stud shooter on right arm

Orange plate reinforces shooter arm

Ganymede is a red cardinal

TWEET TWEET

GANYMEDE

WITH DISPLAY STAND

LEGO BLIZZARD EXCLUSIVE

OMNIC BASTION STATS

Theme	LEGO® Overwatch®
Set name	Omnic Bastion 75987
Pieces	182
Released	2018
Fought	Various

Weapons	
Defence	
Agility	
Speed	

Colours reflect Omnic Crisis game skin

Ganymede stays safe by detaching from Bastion's shoulder when he goes into one of his battle modes.

Torso rotates and limbs fold for sentry mode

Double hinged arms

Very broad feet for stomping and stability

Flat, silver ingots as leg armour

CHAPTER 4
WILD WEAPONS

Some mechs have bigger, badder versions of their owners' weapons. Others rely on number of weapons, hidden weapons or superior firepower. But there's one thing a mech needs just as much as an awesome set of weapons: a pilot with the skill to use them.

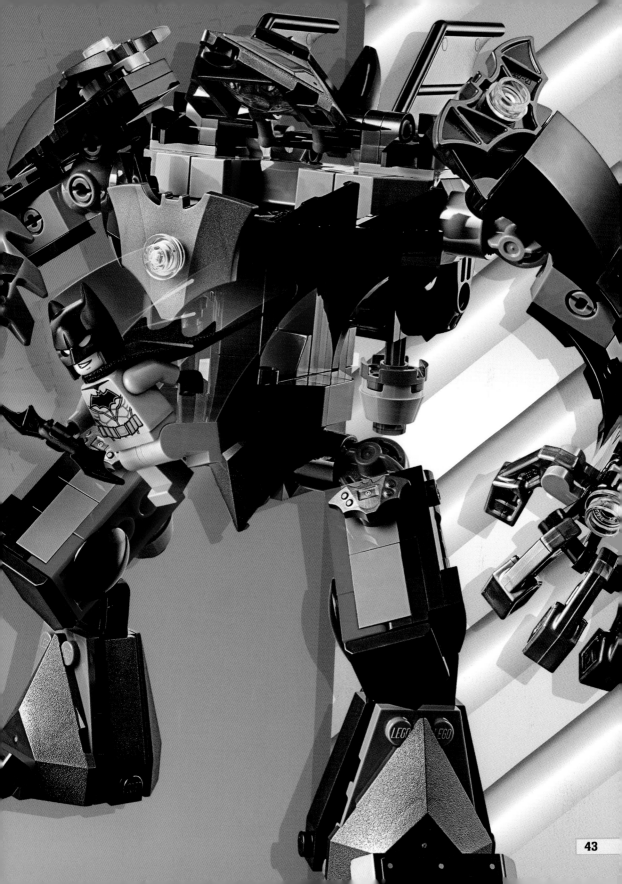

EGGHEAD MECH

Batman's all in a scramble. He's being attacked by Egghead in his egg-shaped mech. It sounds funny, but it's really no yolk. The mech's fried egg cannon could make a mess of Batman's cowl, and its rotating whisk hand could reduce his cape to tatters. Batman's got to stop the mech before it goes free range all over Gotham City!

ALTERNATE VIEW

Egg ammo tank on mech's back

This is one of only 3 mechs in the 32 LEGO® BATMAN MOVIE sets.

THE WHISK CAN ROTATE AND OPEN UP INTO A GRABBING CLAW!

Rotating whisk with grabber claws

Egg missile is round tile with egg yolk print

EGGHEAD MECH STATS

		Weapons						
Theme	THE LEGO® BATMAN MOVIE							
Set name	Egghead™ Mech Food Fight 70920	Defence						
Pieces	293	Agility						
Released	2018	Speed						
Fought	Batman							

I DON'T CRACK THAT EASILY, EGGHEAD!

Chicken laying eggs for fresh ammo

Tube connects tank to egg disk launcher

Dial selects scrambled or fried eggs

PREPARE TO BE SUNNY-SIDE DOWN, BATMAN!

Trigger-operated egg disk launcher

Egghead's accomplice, the Condiment King fires mustard and ketchup.

Egg-shaped cockpit set low down

Short, jointed legs

Big, strutting feet

MECH FILE

Theme	LEGO® Batman
Set	Batman Mech vs. Poison Ivy Mech 76117
Pieces	375
Released	2019

Button-operated flip-up net shooter

Pauldrons lift to allow arms greater range of movement

Bat decorations on pauldrons

Whirling circular saw with extra bat-ended blade

THAT LITTLE MECH LOOKS KIND OF WEEDY, IVY

Dual stud shooters on left wrist

Pointed wedge for pelvis

THE BATMAN MECH'S RIGHT ARM HAS A GRABBING HAND UNDER THE CIRCULAR SAW.

BATTLE STATS

Toes angle up or down to increase posability

Name: Batman Mech
Height: 17 cm (6 in)
Blade power: 8/10
Missiles: 7/10
Trapping power (net): 5/10
Armour: 8/10
Battle rating: 8/10

BATMAN MECH VS. POISON IVY MECH

Right leaf conceals stud shooter

It's a jungle out there! Batman and Poison Ivy are going mech to mech, and Ivy is playing dirty. She's firing toxin-covered studs from a shooter hidden under her flip-up leaf. Ugh! But Batman isn't backing down. Inside the bat-faced cockpit of his hefty mech, he's started his circular saw spinning. Can Batman turn Ivy's vines into shredded greens before she scores a direct hit?

A WELL-AIMED STUD WILL STOP THAT SAW FOR GOOD!

Left leaf conceals minifigure-grabbing vineshooter

IVY HAS NOT BOTHERED WITH A COCKPIT COVER! WILL THIS BE HER DOWNFALL?

Name: Poison Ivy Mech
Height: 13 cm (5 in)
Toxic power: 9/10
Missiles: 6/10
Trapping power (vine): 7/10
Armour: 0/10
Battle rating 7/10

Batman has many enemies, but his mech can handle it. When faced with attacks from above, the Batman Mech fires a net from a secret compartment.

47

REINHARDT MECH

Hammer up! Rockets on! Chaaarrrrge! Part of the Overwatch strike team, Reinhardt battles the omnic robots who menace the world. His mech resembles a suit of armour, but Reinhardt has a weapon no knight ever had: a colossal hammer that runs on rocket power. When the hammer starts swinging, look out!

REINHARDT MECH STATS

Theme	LEGO® Overwatch®
Set name	D.Va & Reinhardt 75973
Pieces	455
Released	2019
Fought	Omnic army

Weapons					
Defence					
Agility					
Speed					

End of hammer can be removed to make a minifigure-size hammer.

THIS SMALL BUT MIGHTY MECH IS **14** CM (5 IN) TALL.

REINHARDT MINIFIGURE

Weapon clips to palm and fingers close

Three exhausts on rocket hammer

Medieval knight–style pauldrons can lift to give more arm movement

MY HAMMER'S A REAL KNOCKOUT

Protective force field emanates from shield

J08 is the name of the armour's maker

A round tile and two bricks with fins form the mech's striking torso armour.

Distinctive pointed foot armour

Ball-jointed ankles

MONKIE KID'S MECH STATS

Theme	LEGO® Monkie Kid™	
Set name	Monkie Kid's Team Secret HQ 80013	
Pieces	1,959	
Released	2020	
Fought	The Bull Clones	

Weapons	
Defence	
Accuracy	
Speed	

THIS BEATS BEING A NOODLE DELIVERY BOY!

Fishing harpoons on shoulders as backup weapons

Hinged elbows

This mech is made up of Monkie Kid's trademark red and gold colours.

Large staff twists and turns to knock out enemies

Ball-jointed hips give freedom of movement

Flat feet with a toe on each side

MONKIE KID MECH

Shhh… Monkie Kid has a secret. Deep in his headquarters, he has been building a mech. It's swift, agile and runs rings around Bull Clones, bopping them on the head with its long, twirling staff. Stud shooters deal with distant enemies, and those who come close might get a poke in the eye from the movable fingers. Nobody messes with the Monkie Kid Mech!

Stud shooters on left arm

Laughing monkey-face sticker

Two grabbing fingers on each hand

Skinny but strong monkey legs

YOU'RE MAKING ME SEE RED!

OUCH... MY HORNS!

GET READY FOR A GORING, NOODLE BOY!

CHAPTER 5
AMAZING ARMOUR

Even fast, agile mechs take a few hits in battle. That's where armour plating comes in. A strong suit of armour can mean the difference between a small dent and a big, battle-stopping injury. When an enemy tests its mettle, a good mech is ready, walking tough and standing steady.

THE SAMURAI MECH

The Skulkin army need to look sharp! Samurai X is after them in her scarlet mech. Will they crumble? They might if the mech's colossal katana makes contact. And if they dodge that, there are two more katanas in its other hand. This mech really is a cut above.

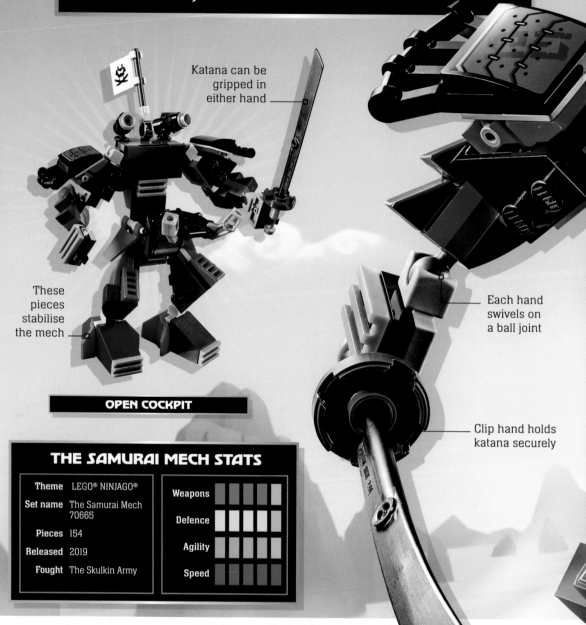

Katana can be gripped in either hand

These pieces stabilise the mech

OPEN COCKPIT

Each hand swivels on a ball joint

Clip hand holds katana securely

THE SAMURAI MECH STATS

Theme	LEGO® NINJAGO®
Set name	The Samurai Mech 70665
Pieces	154
Released	2019
Fought	The Skulkin Army

Weapons	▮▮▮▮▯
Defence	▮▮▮▮▯
Agility	▮▮▮▯▯
Speed	▮▮▮▮▯

Twin blasters mounted on shoulders

Shoulder guards give added protection

TIME TO GRAB A SLICE OF THE ACTION!

Chest plate folds down so Samurai X can hop out

This hand can store spare swords – and act as a sharp claw

Hip armour pieces can be angled up or down

This diminutive but dangerous mech measures 14 cm (5 in) high.

Hammond was genetically modified as part of an experiment. The "8" on the front of his mech indicates that he is Specimen 8.

A turn of a handle makes Hammond pop up!

DON'T CROSS THE HAMSTER...

Pivoting cannons can be angled towards target

Once unfolded, legs can move forwards and back

Orange details make mech hi-vis in battles

WRECKING BALL

This is no ordinary hamster ball! Hammond the Overwatch hero pilots an iron sphere that wrecks rampant robots. It converts into an armour-plated mech. First, Hammond pops up from the cockpit with a steely glare. Then four legs fold out, and the mech starts walking. When the twin quad cannons come out, it's time for foes to flee. Let's roll!

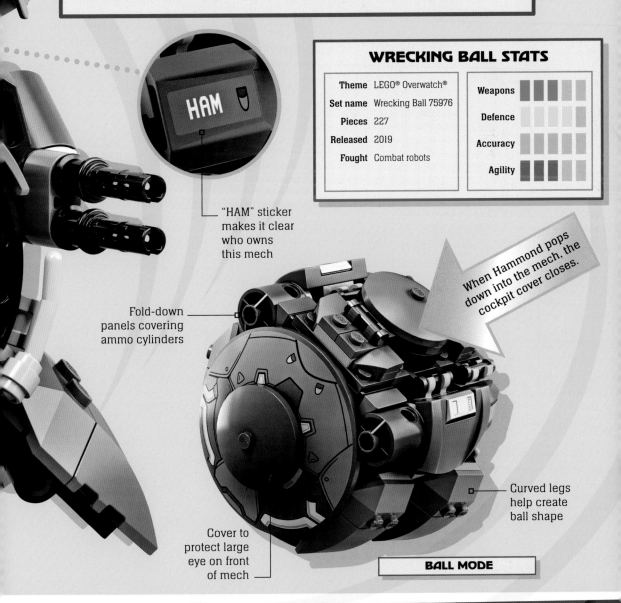

WRECKING BALL STATS

Theme	LEGO® Overwatch®
Set name	Wrecking Ball 75976
Pieces	227
Released	2019
Fought	Combat robots

Weapons	
Defence	
Accuracy	
Agility	

"HAM" sticker makes it clear who owns this mech

Fold-down panels covering ammo cylinders

When Hammond pops down into the mech, the cockpit cover closes.

Curved legs help create ball shape

Cover to protect large eye on front of mech

BALL MODE

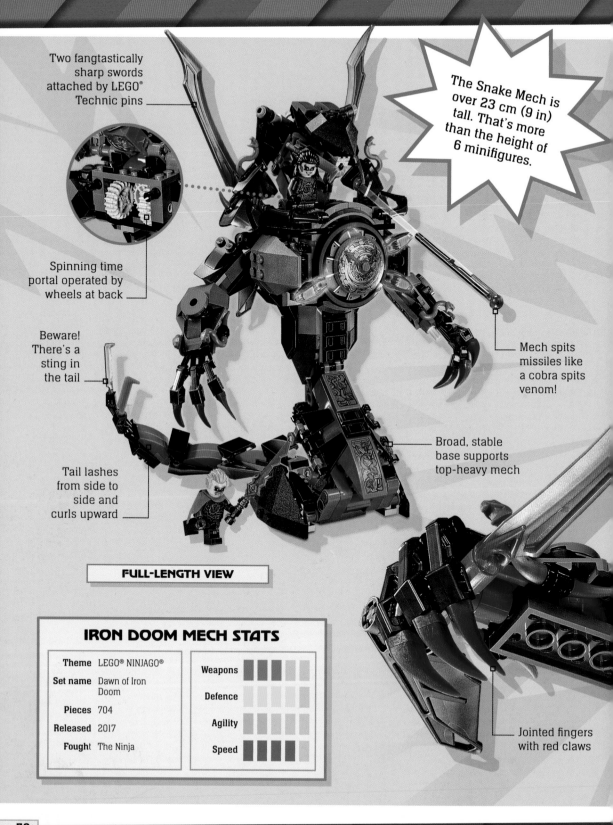

Two fangtastically sharp swords attached by LEGO® Technic pins

The Snake Mech is over 23 cm (9 in) tall. That's more than the height of 6 minifigures.

Spinning time portal operated by wheels at back

Beware! There's a sting in the tail

Tail lashes from side to side and curls upward

Mech spits missiles like a cobra spits venom!

Broad, stable base supports top-heavy mech

FULL-LENGTH VIEW

IRON DOOM MECH STATS

Theme	LEGO® NINJAGO®
Set name	Dawn of Iron Doom
Pieces	704
Released	2017
Fought	The Ninja

Weapons
Defence
Agility
Speed

Jointed fingers with red claws

SNAKE MECH

Snakes alive! There's a battle going on in the swamp. The Time Twins have had the Vermillion warriors build a giant snake mech, and it's attacking the Ninja. Its giant eye fires missiles, its arms are protected by armor and hold multiple weapons and it can even time travel thanks to a whirling time portal. Yikes! Have Jay and Lloyd met their doom?

Snake head raises to reveal missile-shooting eye

Double cockpit for Time Twins Acronix and Krux

SNAKE IT 'TIL YOU MAKE IT... THAT'S OUR MOTTO.

Mini red snake decorations on shoulder armor

There are four Time Blades to collect, and this is the only set that includes them all.

Time portal has plug-in points for 4 Time Blades

CHAPTER 6
VEHICLE MECHS

A vehicle can be a real game changer. Naturally it can zip a mech to the battlefield super fast, but that's not all. Imagine a flyer unexpectedly detaching from a mech, or a mech suddenly reconfiguring into a scooter. What a way to mess up an enemy's battle plan!

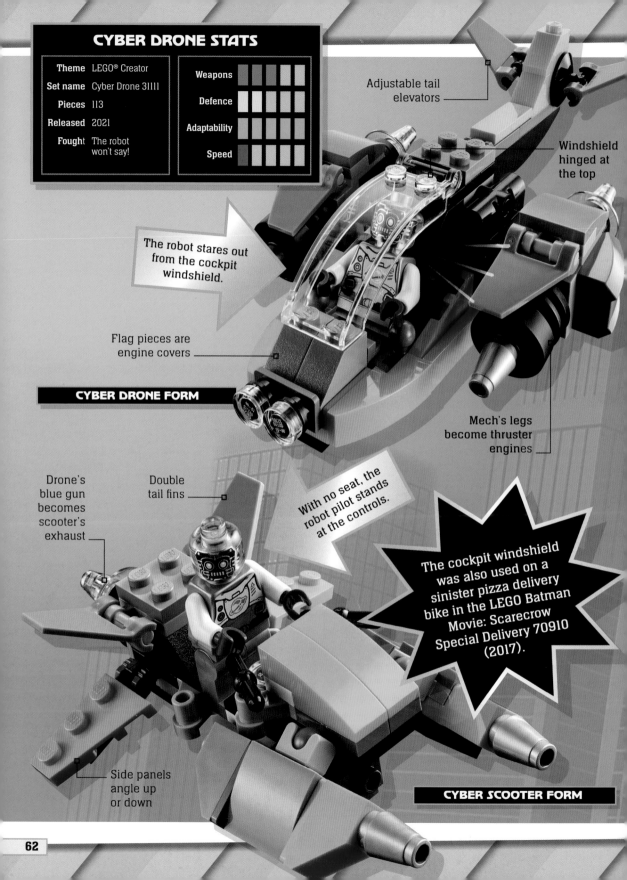

CYBER DRONE STATS

Theme	LEGO® Creator	**Weapons**	■ ■ □ □ □
Set name	Cyber Drone 31111	**Defence**	■ □ □ □ □
Pieces	113	**Adaptability**	■ ■ ■ □ □
Released	2021	**Speed**	■ ■ ■ ■ □
Fought	The robot won't say!		

Adjustable tail elevators

Windshield hinged at the top

The robot stares out from the cockpit windshield.

Flag pieces are engine covers

CYBER DRONE FORM

Mech's legs become thruster engines

Drone's blue gun becomes scooter's exhaust

Double tail fins

With no seat, the robot pilot stands at the controls.

The cockpit windshield was also used on a sinister pizza delivery bike in the LEGO Batman Movie: Scarecrow Special Delivery 70910 (2017).

Side panels angle up or down

CYBER SCOOTER FORM

CYBER DRONE

The 3 in 1 Cyber Drone is the ultimate convertible. As a drone, it can fly to outer space. When rebuilt as a scooter, it whizzes along at ground level. And in mech form it stomps the Earth, blaster at the ready. Is the robot pilot up to no good, or is he here to save the world? He's bleeping that to himself for now!

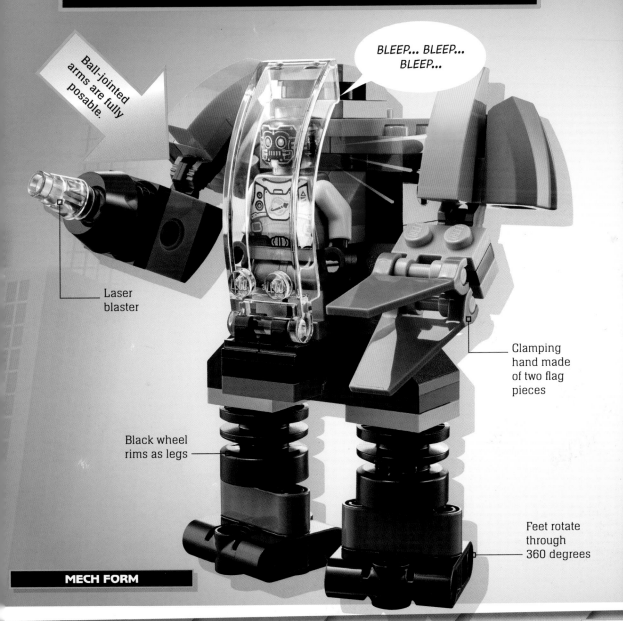

Ball-jointed arms are fully posable.

BLEEP... BLEEP... BLEEP...

Laser blaster

Clamping hand made of two flag pieces

Black wheel rims as legs

Feet rotate through 360 degrees

MECH FORM

Yellow
QUAKE and
gorilla flags
fly high

Four
concealed
soundwave
shooters
on each
shoulder

Yellow lights
look like
glaring eyes

Huge, booming
loudspeakers
on shoulders

WANT ME
TO TURN
THE TUNES UP?

DARN NINJAS
AND THEIR LOUD
ROCK MUSIC!

WARNING

Stabiliser on
wheel so mech
doesn't topple
when hit

This stocky mech
is almost as wide
as it is tall. It stands
at 33 cm (12 in)
high and 30 cm
(11 in) wide.

QUAKE MECH

Cole's Quake Mech uses sound to make foes shake. Sounds unlikely? The Shark Army thought so, too. But now they're wobbling all over the place in the blast from the mech's loudspeakers. A sound missile smack in the gills doesn't help! Maybe they should release that reporter they've captured and sound the retreat.

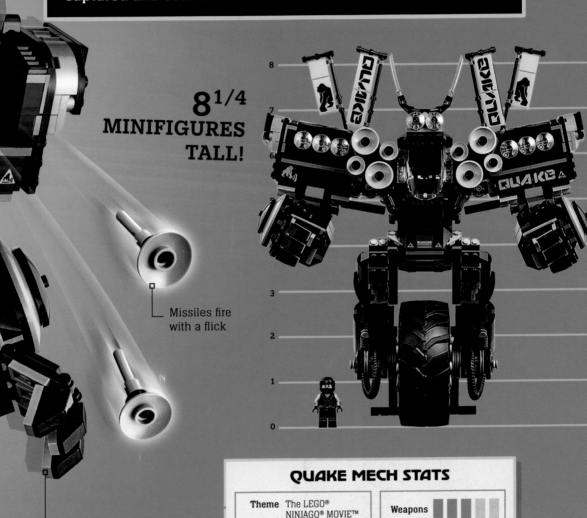

8 1/4 MINIFIGURES TALL!

Missiles fire with a flick

Giant, gripping fists

QUAKE MECH STATS

Theme	The LEGO® NINJAGO® MOVIE™
Set name	Quake Mech 70632
Pieces	1,202
Released	2017
Fought	Garmadon's Shark Army

Weapons	▮▮□□□
Defence	▮□□□□
Agility	▮▮□□□
Speed	▮▮▮▮▮

KAI'S MECH JET

Jet plane incoming! Kai's flown into the Prime Empire video game to sort out some sinister goings on. But wait – the plane rebuilds into a giant mech. Can it grab the Key-Tana and beat the game? It must knock out the enemy Whack Rat with its stud shooters first. Time for some top-level battle action...

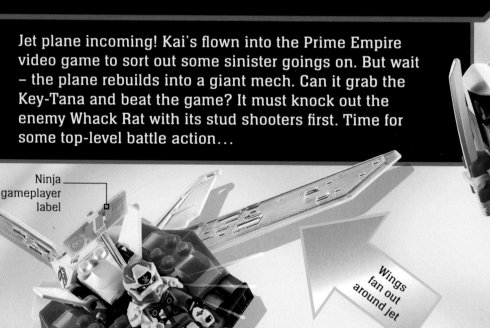

Ninja gameplayer label

Wings fan out around jet

Joystick is game controller

KAI'S JET VIEW

Collectible trans-orange Key-Tana

YAH... I'M GOING FULL WHACK ON YOU!

There are two more trans-orange Key-Tanas to collect; one in set 71713 Empire Dragon and the other in set 71712 Empire Temple of Madness.

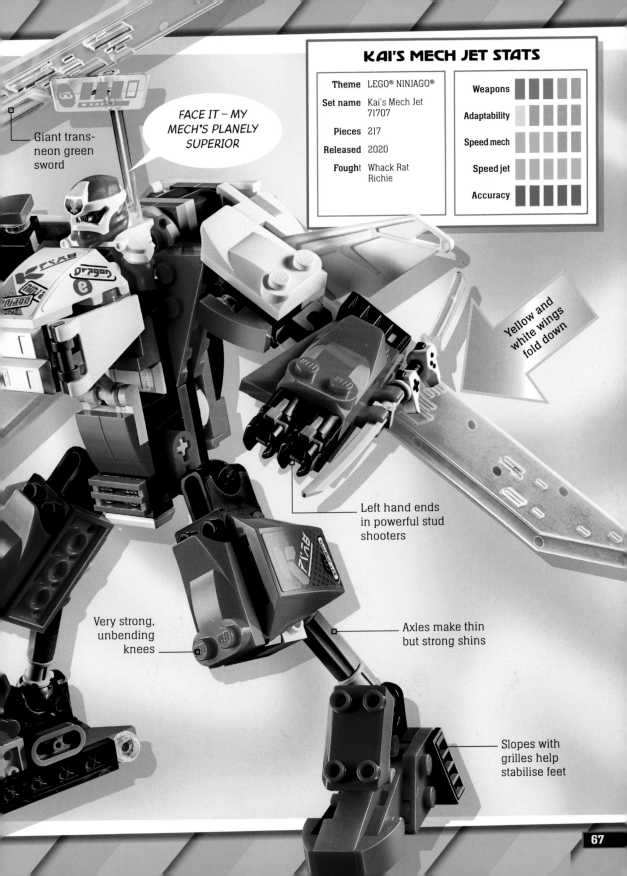

Giant trans-neon green sword

FACE IT – MY MECH'S PLANELY SUPERIOR

KAI'S MECH JET STATS

Theme	LEGO® NINJAGO®				
Set name	Kai's Mech Jet 71707				
Pieces	217				
Released	2020				
Fought	Whack Rat Richie				

Weapons					
Adaptability					
Speed mech					
Speed jet					
Accuracy					

Yellow and white wings fold down

Left hand ends in powerful stud shooters

Very strong, unbending knees

Axles make thin but strong shins

Slopes with grilles help stabilise feet

THUNDER RAIDER

Who's that super-size hitchhiker on board the Thunder Raider? It's Ninja Cole's mighty mech! The mech takes a backseat while the vehicle is moving, but beware – those shooters can fold forwards for on-road action. Once the mech detaches, it's blasting time. But can the mech's missiles blunt the Overlord's chainsaw?

The mech blends seamlessly into the Thunder Raider. Villains get a shock when the mech springs into action!

Cole watches out for approaching villains.

Treads made of large links with pinholes

Huge, grippy wheel with gold rim

TRANSPORT MODE

Orange spring-loaded shooters

Cole's gorilla symbol on shoulder

YOU NEED TO SHARPEN UP YOUR ACT, OVERLORD

Two gold katanas on each hand

Black and gold colours of the Earth Ninja

Shin guards with stickers

Feet clip together to form stable base

YOU'RE DRIVING ME CRAZY, NINJA

THUNDER RAIDER STATS

Theme	LEGO® NINJAGO®		Weapons					
Set name	Thunder Raider 71699		Defence					
Pieces	576		Agility					
Released	2020		Speed					
Fought	The Overlord							

69

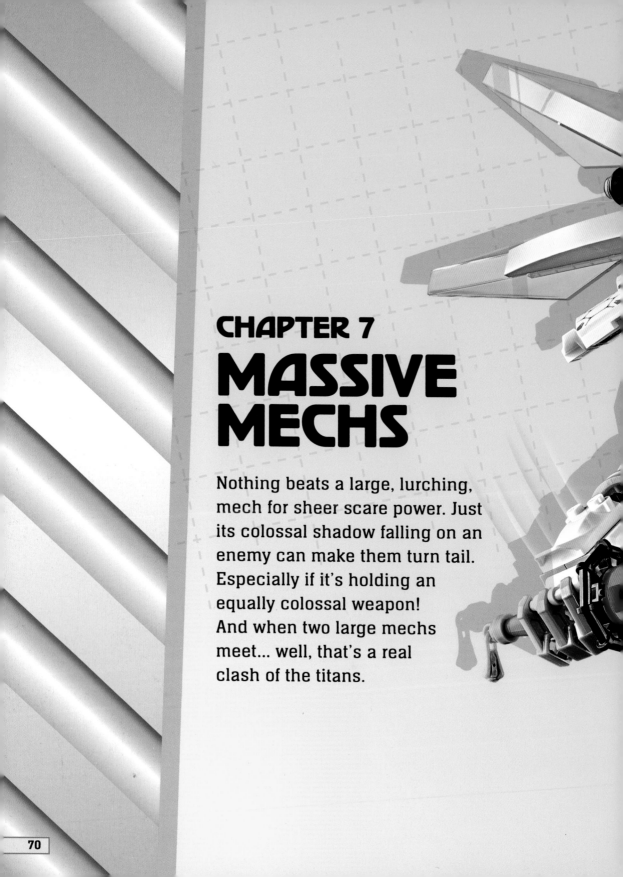

CHAPTER 7
MASSIVE MECHS

Nothing beats a large, lurching, mech for sheer scare power. Just its colossal shadow falling on an enemy can make them turn tail. Especially if it's holding an equally colossal weapon! And when two large mechs meet... well, that's a real clash of the titans.

GOLDEN MECH

Stomp, stomp, STOMP! The Stone Army is on the march. But Lloyd is coming for them in his Golden Mech, and it has a gigantic katana in its hand. Lloyd is well protected; he's almost invisible under the fold-down cockpit canopy. Whoosh! The mech's posable arm rises high in the air. Those stone warriors will be reduced to rubble in no time!

GOLDEN MECH STATS

Theme	LEGO® NINJAGO®	
Set name	Golden Mech 71702	
Pieces	489	
Released	2020	
Fought	The Stone Army	

Weapons	
Defence	
Agility	
Speed	

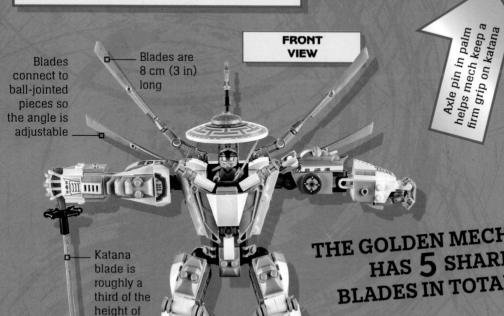

Katana hilt is an octagonal ring

Fingers splay and fold around katana handle

Axle pin in palm helps mech keep a firm grip on katana

FRONT VIEW

Blades connect to ball-jointed pieces so the angle is adjustable

Blades are 8 cm (3 in) long

Katana blade is roughly a third of the height of the mech

THE GOLDEN MECH HAS 5 SHARP BLADES IN TOTAL

Stops on front and back of foot prevent ankle from overflexing

Having a concealed cockpit is an unusual feature for a LEGO mech. It's likely to give Lloyd an edge in battle!

CRUMBLING ALREADY, STONE ARMY?

Broad cockpit canopy is a radar dish and conical hat

Pauldrons look like temple roof tiles

Fan-shaped crest made of golden propellor blades

Ratcheted hip joints give chunky legs great posability

Elbow can bend backwards as well as forwards

Jointed knees enable mech to kneel for ground level fighting

BATTLE STATS

Name: Monkey King Warrior Mech
Height: 40 cm (15 in)
Agility: 8/10
Missiles: 0/10
Bashing power: 9/10
Armour: 5/10
Battle rating: 8/10

Name: Demon Bull King Mech
Height: 29 cm (11 in)
Agility: 4/10
Missiles: 5/10
Fire power: 8/10
Slicing power: 6/10
Battle rating: 7/10

Monkey head turns up, down and from side to side

Chest opens to reveal cockpit

Adjustable Monkie Kid flags

Beware the fearsome flame thrower!

Elbow pads shield against missiles

Monkie Kid can ride in the mech's palm

WHO SAYS YOU SHOULDN'T SHOW RED TO A BULL?

Extendable staff ideal for bull-bashing!

Feet look like gigantic cloven hooves

MONKIE KID'S LARGE RED CAPE IS UNIQUE TO SET 80012.

Rotating feet with upturned toe armour

DEMON BULL KING VS. MONKEY KING

Demon Bull King is smashing up the city. That's made Monkie Kid see red! In his massive Monkey King Mech with its giant staff, he could make mincemeat of the big bully, if he can just dodge the spinning flame thrower. Ready, steady, chaaaarge!

Shoulder-mounted lava stud shooters

Huge axe with multiple orange blades

THE EVIL PRINCESS IRON FAN CAN RIDE ON THE BACK OF THE MECH.

Button-operated light brick makes torso glow

HOPE YOU'RE A FAN OF MY MECH, MONKIE KID!

Fixed knees for stability

MECH FILE

Theme	LEGO® Monkie Kid™
Set	Demon Bull King 80010
Pieces	1375
Released	2020

ZANE'S TITAN MECH

Who's afraid of ghost warriors? Not Ninja Zane! Ghouls don't stand a chance against his massive Titan Mech. The ice-white mech is enough to put a shiver up anyone's spine. It has a sword in one hand, a spinning chainsaw in the other, and stud shooters on the shoulders. When the Titan Mech arrives, it's time for ghosts to disappear.

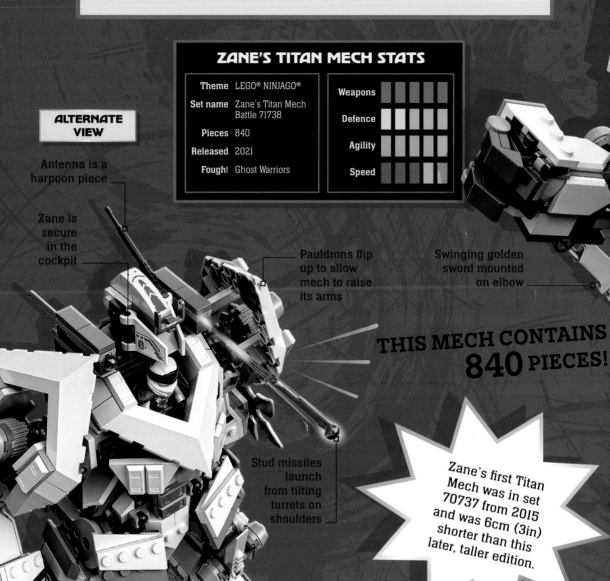

ZANE'S TITAN MECH STATS

Theme	LEGO® NINJAGO®
Set name	Zane's Titan Mech Battle 71738
Pieces	840
Released	2021
Fought	Ghost Warriors

Weapons					
Defence					
Agility					
Speed					

ALTERNATE VIEW

Antenna is a harpoon piece

Zane is secure in the cockpit

Pauldrons flip up to allow mech to raise its arms

Swinging golden sword mounted on elbow

Stud missiles launch from tilting turrets on shoulders

THIS MECH CONTAINS **840** PIECES!

Zane's first Titan Mech was in set 70737 from 2015 and was 6cm (3in) shorter than this later, taller edition.

Arms rotate through 360 degrees

Shuriken-style chainsaw spins at devastating speed

Hip panels lift to allow full range of leg movement

Bendable knees increase poseability

FEELING COLD, SOUL ARCHER? YOU'RE TREMBLING!

Hidden thrusters behind ankle panels

FREEZE, NINJA!

MONKIE KID VS. THE BONE DEMON

Monkie Kid's little red mech is on his high-flying cloud board, and he's getting right in the face of the blustering bone mech. The Monkie mech can't match the bone mech for power, but speed and agility are on its side. "Doink" goes its staff, right in the skeleton's cockpit cranium. Time to rattle some bones!

Staff with gold tassles on each end

Posable hand

Swords attached to palms of hands

Hoverboard known as a cloud board

Monkie kid needs to avoid these spiky tooth pieces

Bone demon sits in the bony cockpit

I'LL KNOCK YOU OFF THAT CLOUD BOARD, MONKIE KID!

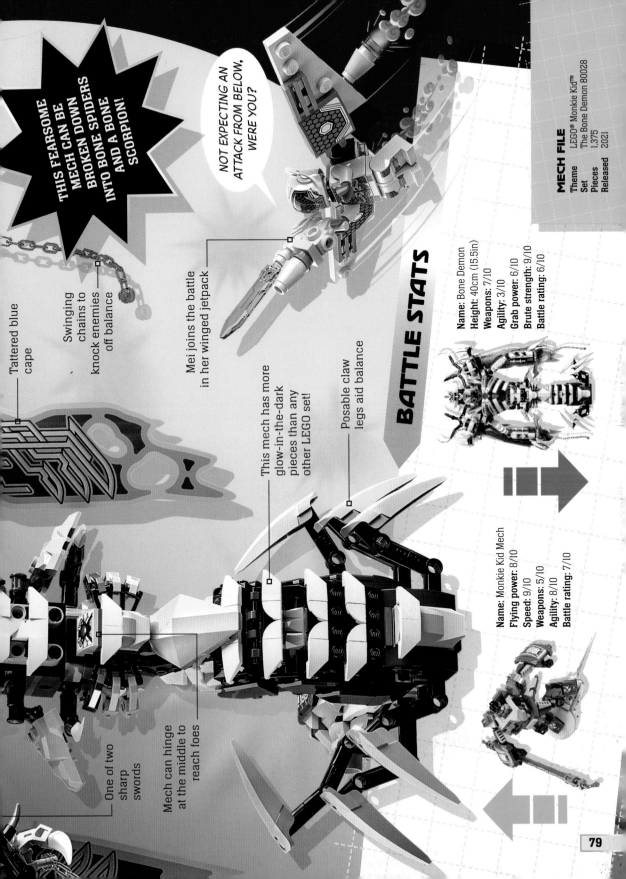

THIS FEARSOME MECH CAN BE BROKEN DOWN INTO BONE SPIDERS AND A BONE SCORPION!

NOT EXPECTING AN ATTACK FROM BELOW, WERE YOU?

Tattered blue cape

Swinging chains to knock enemies off balance

Mei joins the battle in her winged jetpack

This mech has more glow-in-the-dark pieces than any other LEGO set!

Posable claw legs aid balance

One of two sharp swords

Mech can hinge at the middle to reach foes

MECH FILE

Theme	LEGO® Monkie Kid™
Set	The Bone Demon 80028
Pieces	1,375
Released	2021

BATTLE STATS

Name: Bone Demon
Height: 40cm (15.5in)
Weapons: 7/10
Agility: 3/10
Grab power: 6/10
Brute strength: 9/10
Battle rating: 6/10

Name: Monkie Kid Mech
Flying power: 8/10
Speed: 9/10
Weapons: 5/10
Agility: 8/10
Battle rating: 7/10

This section can detach to act as a flyer

Transparent green blades

Sword handles decorate the mech's head

STOP GIVING ME THE COLD SHOULDER, NINJA!

This is Lloyd's second mech. The first was his Golden Mech from 70505 Temple of Light in 2013.

Hip joints for movability

LLOYD'S TITAN MECH

With the Blizzard samurai causing havoc, Lloyd needs a mighty mech that can do battle in extreme weather conditions. Enter the Titan Mech! Highly posable and packed with awesome weapons, this mech is sure to strike fear into the heart of the iciest foe. It even has a detachable flyer so Lloyd can chase flighty foes.

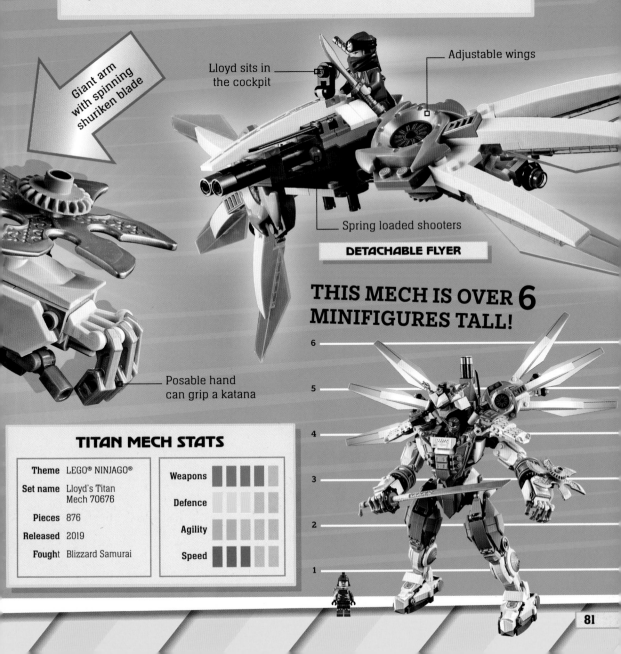

Giant arm with spinning shuriken blade

Lloyd sits in the cockpit

Adjustable wings

Spring loaded shooters

DETACHABLE FLYER

Posable hand can grip a katana

THIS MECH IS OVER 6 MINIFIGURES TALL!

6
5
4
3
2
1

TITAN MECH STATS

Theme	LEGO® NINJAGO®
Set name	Lloyd's Titan Mech 70676
Pieces	876
Released	2019
Fought	Blizzard Samurai

Weapons

Defence

Agility

Speed

GLOSSARY

Agility – The ability to move around and change direction quickly

Cockpit – The area in a mech or vehicle where the pilot sits and operates the controls

Convertible – A vehicle that can change shape

Diminutive – Small

Harpoon – A long spear-like tool that is normally used to catch large fish or whales

Hydraulic – Powered by water

Katana – A single-edged sword

Missile – Something that is fired at an enemy, for example out of a cannon

Pauldron – A piece of armour that covers the shoulder

Pincers – A clawlike tool that can grip things

Pivot – To turn around

Samurai – A specially trained warrior

Sentient – Having feelings and awareness

Recon – A mission to explore a particular place

Sentry – Standing guard

Shuriken – A throwing weapon with three points

Tandem – Separate things working in partnership with each other

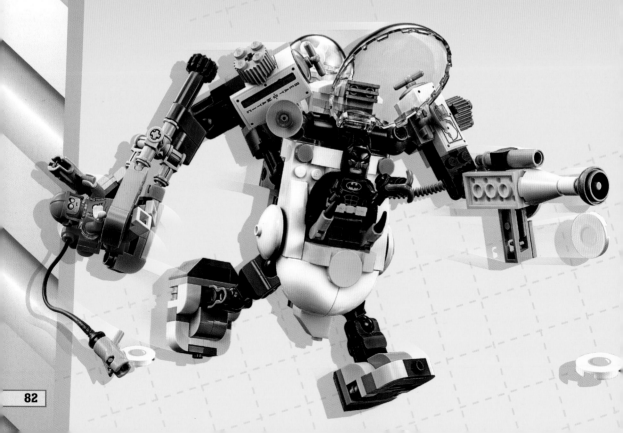

Project Editor Rosie Peet
Senior Designer Anne Sharples
Designer Thelma Jane Robb
Production Editor Siu Yin Chan
Senior Controller Louise Minihane
Managing Editor Paula Regan
Managing Art Editor Jo Connor
Publishing Director Mark Searle

Written by Julia March

Dorling Kindersley would like to thank: Randi Sørensen,
Heidi K. Jensen, Paul Hansford, and Martin Leighton
Lindhardt at the LEGO Group; Benjamin Harper at
Warner Bros; Byron Parnell at Blizzard; Megan Startz at
Universal; Julia March for indexing; Nicole Reynolds for
editorial assistance and Megan Douglass for proofreading.

First published in Great Britain in 2021 by
Dorling Kindersley Limited
DK, One Embassy Gardens, 8 Viaduct Gardens,
London SW11 7BW

The authorised representative in the EEA is
Dorling Kindersley Verlag GmbH. Arnulfstr. 124,
80636 Munich, Germany

Page design copyright ©2021 Dorling Kindersley Limited
A Penguin Random House Company

10 9 8 7 6 5 4 3 2 1
001–325539–Oct/21

A CIP catalogue record for this book
is available from the British Library.
ISBN: 978-0-24152-178-6

Printed and bound in China

For the curious
www.LEGO.com
www.dk.com